QUILTING DESIGNS FROM Nature

Lone J. Minkkinen

American Quilter's Society

P. O. Box 3290 • Paducah, KY 42002-3290
www.AmericanQuilter.com

Located in Paducah, Kentucky, the American Quilter's Society (AQS) is dedicated to promoting the accomplishments of today's quilters. Through its publications and events, AQS strives to honor today's quiltmakers and their work and to inspire future creativity and innovation in quiltmaking.

EXECUTIVE BOOK EDITOR: ANDI MILAM REYNOLDS
SENIOR BOOK EDITOR: LINDA BAXTER LASCO
COPY EDITOR: CHRYSTAL ABHALTER
GRAPHIC DESIGN: LYNDA SMITH
COVER DESIGN: MICHAEL BUCKINGHAM

Additional copies of this book may be ordered from the American Quilter's Society, PO Box 3290, Paducah, KY 42002-3290, or online at www.AmericanQuilter.com.

Text & Patterns © 2011, Author, Lone J. Minkkinen
Book Design © 2011, American Quilter's Society

Library of Congress Cataloging-in-Publication Data

Minkkinen, Lone J.
    Quilting designs from nature / by Lone J. Minkkinen.
        p. cm.
    ISBN 978-1-60460-001-8
    1. Quilting--Patterns. 2. Nature in art. I. Title.
    TT835.M569 2011
    746.46'041--dc22
                                          2011015234

Dinosaur photo courtesy of TaylorMadeFossils.com

Dedication

To Amanda, my clear Moonbeam

To Jeffrey, my shining Sunray

And to Jim, the Bridge Builder
The years with you have been the best of my life.

Acknowledgments

Being the lucky person I am in knowing many wonderful and humorous personalities, there are some I would like to mention for touching my journey in making this book:

Aileen Clark, you introduced me to quilting and showed me your beautiful quilts, and later gently suggested using a rotary cutter instead of scissors for cutting fabrics. Best tip I ever got!

Amanda, thank you for the charming way you explain American words and phrases. Your dry sense of humor and our common interest in words are very important to me. Thanks for always being open with a tip on fashion or style.

Andi Reynolds, who spotted a single sheep among hounds and horses. I never would have thought this little woolen ewe could be the beginning of my very first book. Thanks Andi!

My friend, Dr. Barb, the way you lovingly make and give quilts to all who are dear to you reminds me that all the hours and thoughts with which we embellish our quilts are the true reward of this craftsmanship. Your unusual but always stylish choices of color are an inspiration.

Bedste and Arki, thank you for tending to the Danish cottage and garden at home, and for showing me that it is the little things in life that make it grand. You are the proof of why Danes are considered to be the happiest people in the world. Nobody enjoys a hot cup of coffee on a sunny summer day the way you do.

Jan Stebbins, my fellow artist and true friend, your voice is like a calming drug when things seems to melt together. We can't unscramble the eggs, but we sure can serve them with salsa!

Jean Wheatly, thank you for sharing your masterpiece of a garden with me. I have enjoyed those special times sitting in the golf cart with you, watching dusk descend over the clover field, and having long conversations of important things such as life in a beehive. The fierceness with which you overcome hardships has taught me so much. I value our friendship greatly.

Jeffrey, placing your fantastic Lego® creations on my sketching table has indeed been inspiring. Tucking your red shark ever so gently between the window and the Do-Not-Touch-Table as a happy decoration for me to see when looking up from my drawings has made my day. Thank you, Buddy!

When thanking and acknowledging the people in my life, the first and foremost on my mind is my husband, Jim. You have the brightest mind and the kindest heart. It was a good day when we met. Thank you for never once questioning how much fabric is enough. And you can always count on me to locate the mustard or find your lost glasses.

To my canine personal trainers, Roscoe and Nacho, seeing the leashes in my hand fires you up every time. Your enthusiasm is contagious. Though I rescued you from the shelter, it turns out you were the ones saving me.

To my horse Shamrock, for carrying me through trillium and belly high ferns, and bravely dodging an occasional horse-eating rock. Our adventures together on the trails are experiences to remember.

Table of Contents

The Barn Yard   7

Two Lambs, Hen & Rooster, Ewe & Ram (1), Ewe & Ram (2), Sheep 'n Stars (border), Wheat (1), Wheat (2), Pears, Piglet

The Pond   16

Frog on Lily Pad (block), Dragonfly (block), Frog/Lilypad with Dragonflies (block), Frogs with Dragonflies (border), Dragonfly with Frogs (border), Dragonfly (block), Lizard, Pond Lily

The Ocean   25

Seahorse, Fish, Seahorse with Shells (block), Seahorses with Twirls (block), Seahorses with Coral (border), Seahorses with Twirls (border), Seashell (1), Mussel & Seashell (2), Dolphin

The Forest   34

Oak Leaves and Acorn (1), Beetle & Moth, Oak Leaves and Acorn (2), Mushrooms, Chanterelles, Boxing Hares, Fig Leaves, Deer, Two Butterflies

The Dogs   44

German Shepherd & Westie, Jack Russell & Maltese, Schnauzer & Pug, Labrador & Dachshund, Beagle & Tennis Balls, Chihuahua & Basset Hound, Sheepdog, Great Dane, Heinz 57, Heinz 58

The Birds   56

Song Bird with Music, California Quail, Swan, Owl on Tree Trunk & Great Horned Owl, Four Little Owls, Puffin & Two Penguins, Flamingo Island, Sitting Eagle, Soaring Eagle

The Flowers   65

Day Dream, Honeysuckle, Wild Rose (block 1), Wild Rose (triangle), Wild Rose (rectangle), Violet, Midsummer, Wild Rose (block 2), Lily

Equestrian   74

Crop & English Saddle, Bridle & English Top Hat, Western Boot, Saddle & Hat, Rearing Horse, Trotting Foal, Horse Face, Galloping Horse, Horse Face/Shoe (block/border)

Dinosaurs, Dragons & More   83

Dino (1), Dino (2), Dragon (the whole thing), Dragon (front), Dragon (middle), Dragon (wing), Dragon (tail), Dragon Face, Pegasus, Texas Longhorn, Teapot, Cupcake & Teacup

About the Author

Introduction

About Cake and Quilting

Imagine a child eating chocolate cake. All senses are focused on that decadent, rich, and flavorful piece on the plate. He eats with both his eyes and mouth; you can almost see how the taste buds explode with joy every time the fork lifts yet another bite into the mouth. There is nothing in this world other than the boy and his cake. He has no thoughts about what's for dinner or if he should ride his bicycle or skateboard next. Just him and his cake; it is a perfect moment.

It is similar to a quiltmaker savoring every delicious step along the way until the final binding is attached—not worrying about how long it takes or thinking about the next quilt waiting to be made. Another perfect moment.

When we are not satisfied, we take the time to rip and redo, knowing that we will be happier once our piece is completed even if it takes extra time. Each and every quilter adds his/her personal style to their work. For some, a little crooked seam is all OK, while for others a straight seam is an absolute must. That is what makes handmade quilts unique.

Whatever your preferences are, I hope this book and its various inhabitants will be useful for making your quilts just the way you want them to be. And remember to enjoy every delicious step along the way, even snipping off loose threads.

It is truly a luxury and a blessing to be a quilt-maker!

Before You Quilt

Make a little scrap quilt from the strips and pieces you have left from cutting fabrics for your new project. Sandwich this little scrap quilt model with batting and light fabric for backing. Next, quilt it together to see how the choices of thread work with the different fabrics. It is also an opportunity to adjust your machine to the correct tension. It warms up your hands and gets your mind in the quilting mode.

Later this little test quilt can be fussy cut into 4" x 6" postcards. Sew a blanket stitch around the edge and you will have a miniature quilt to send to someone special.

Changing the Size of the Design

When deciding on which design to use, especially when enlarging, keep in mind the recommended quilting distance suggested by the manufacturer of your batting.

When reducing sizes, some lines can be too tight together. That problem can be fixed by increasing design space when transferring to quilting paper.

I like to use the zoom function on a copy machine for changing sizes. Here is a little piece of EASY math to find the correct zoom percentage to make your copy:

Measure the size you want the design to be. Let's call this measurement Q. Then measure the actual size of the design. Let's call this measurement Z.

When changing inches to numbers on your calculator, use decimals, for example:

¼" = 0.25
½" = 0.50
¾" = 0.75

Multiply $100 \times Q = Y$

Divide Y by Z = % (percent) to reduce/enlarge design. Round off to an even number.

Let's say you have decided to use the Dragonfly block on page 18, which is 7". The block you want it fitted into is 8½".

Then you will calculate $100 \times 8.50 = 850$. Then divide 850 by 7, and your percentage to enlarge this block will be 121.4 %. Round off and set the copier zoom to 121% for your desired pattern size.

Pattern Navigation

◄ = Start   ◄ = Stop   ◄ = Continue design

Transferring Designs to Quilt Top

There are several ways you can draw quilting designs on your quilt top. Before marking your quilt, always make sure the pens that you will be using are of washable ink. If you choose self-disappearing markers, test that the ink actually disappears after a while. Use on a scrap piece of fabric before you begin.

When planning the entire quilting layout, it is helpful to start by placing the bigger blocks of designs. Then you can see which spaces need to be filled in and connect your main designs. You can echo quilt, do free-style swirls, or stitch in the ditch. Quilted "channels" complement most designs and make the quilt more resistant to wear and tear. Mixing hand and machine quilting usually doesn't come out right, but an option that will fit both styles is to simply tie the "bare" spaces with a matching thread.

Here are a few suggestions:

Quilting paper or tissue paper

My preferred method is to transfer the design onto quilting paper or tissue paper with a pencil and pin it to the sandwiched quilt. This way you can move your objects around and the paper is transparent enough to see the blocks underneath. Be sure to move the pin-basting safety pins so you don't break the needle when quilting.

Instead of tracing the design numerous times when you plan to repeat the design, make copies using your sewing machine and an unthreaded needle. Simply trace the design once and sew through up to four layers of paper. Position the perforated paper on the quilt top and quilt along the perforated lines.

Chalk pounce

An alternative to quilting through quilting paper is to mark the perforated design with a chalk pounce. Remove the paper and quilt along the chalk-marked lines.

Light box

With smaller projects such as wallhangings or "quilt as you go," use a light box and a quilt marking pen or chalk. Tape the design onto a light box, place the quilt over it, right-side up, and you'll be able to see the design through the fabric. Trace the design onto the fabric.

Light boxes are widely available at craft and art supply stores.

Needle and Thread

Just like a painter changes paintbrushes for different strokes, you need to change the needle on your machine to match the thread and sewing technique. Ask at your local sewing store or study some of the informative books on the market. I recommend Sarah Ann Smith's book, *Threadwork Unraveled*, by AQS.

Remember to change the needle frequently. Do not wait until it breaks or starts making a popping sound. If the needle gets too dull it can actually rip your fabric. Sometimes I wish my machine had an odometer tracking how many inches I have sewn, but unfortunately it doesn't. It is time to change the needle after every 6 to 7 hours of actual sewing time when sewing through the two layers of fabric, batting, and paper design.

When picking thread, be as specific as when buying fabrics. The varieties of not only colors, but also textures and thicknesses, are too numerous to mention in this book. Go on your own safari in the Jungle of Threads. You will find much helpful advice at your fabric store and there also is a lot of literature about this subject.

When picking a color for your thread, there are always the safe choices of using either clear nylon thread or picking the same color family as the patchwork. Either a solid or a variegated thread can achieve a coordinated, wholesome look. When you want the quilting work to really stand out, the use of metallic threads can be an excellent option.

Colors work with each other in many different ways. Warm-colored threads (reds, yellows, golds), stand out when paired with cool-colored fabrics (blues, greens). Red and blue colors compete, but in the right amounts and hues, result in a wonderful combination. Brown and orange colors dance slowly together, while crisp white and deep blue make a clean and fresh appearance. Pink and brown work together like wool batting, warm and fuzzy.

Make your own observations and experiments, and do not start on the actual quilt until you are absolutely satisfied with your test quilt.

Tips and Haberdashery

✓ Before I wash my new fabrics, I cut a little triangle off each corner. This prevents the fabrics from fraying too much.

✓ Instead of drying the wet fabrics in the dryer, hang them up outside the old-fashioned way, preferably on a windy day. It saves energy, and leaves no annoying creases like the dryer method often does.

✓ Place the ironing board in another room, or even better, on another floor from your sewing machine. Also, every time you sit down or stand up from you chair, try to do one or two squats. Doing so adds up at the end of the day, and doesn't feel like a big effort to get in a little exercise while working on your quilt.

✓ A lint roller can be handy for picking up leftover pieces from your quilting paper, and it does a neat job.

The Barn Yard

One ram per twenty ewes is PLENTY. Otherwise, you could be asking for trouble. Also, in the chapter on Dogs you'll find a trained sheepdog. He'll keep them all in line.

Two Lambs

Ewe & Ram

Sheep 'n Stars

Start at any point
on the design

Wheat

Pears

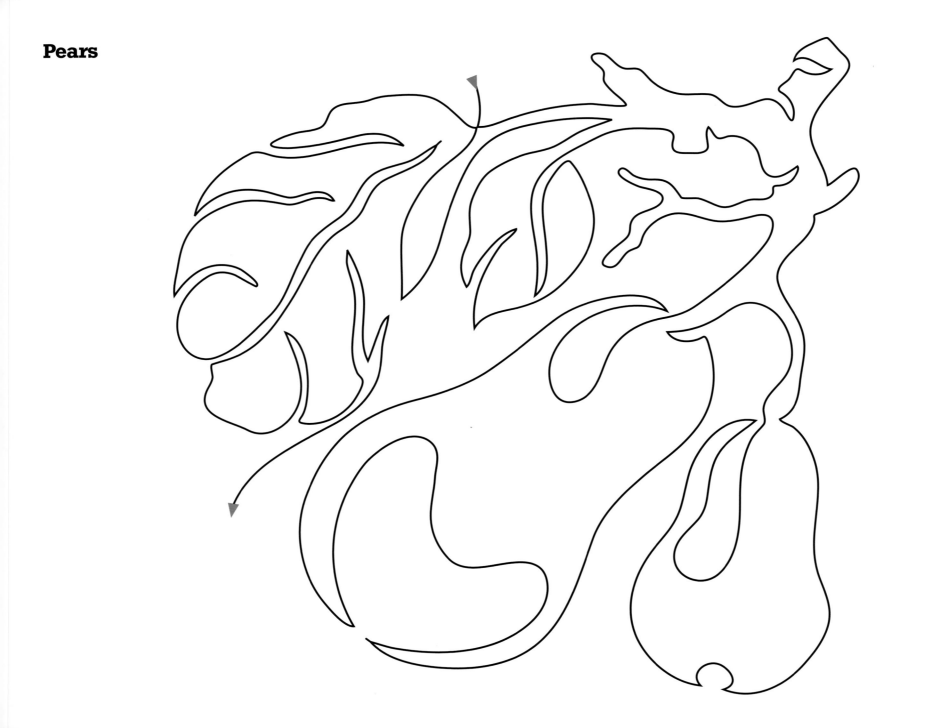

The Pond

The buzzing and quaking of the pond is a sure sign of summer—
prehistoric dragonflies and frogs lead the choir!

Dragonfly

Start at any point
on the design

Frog/Lilypad with Dragonflies

Dragonfly with Frogs

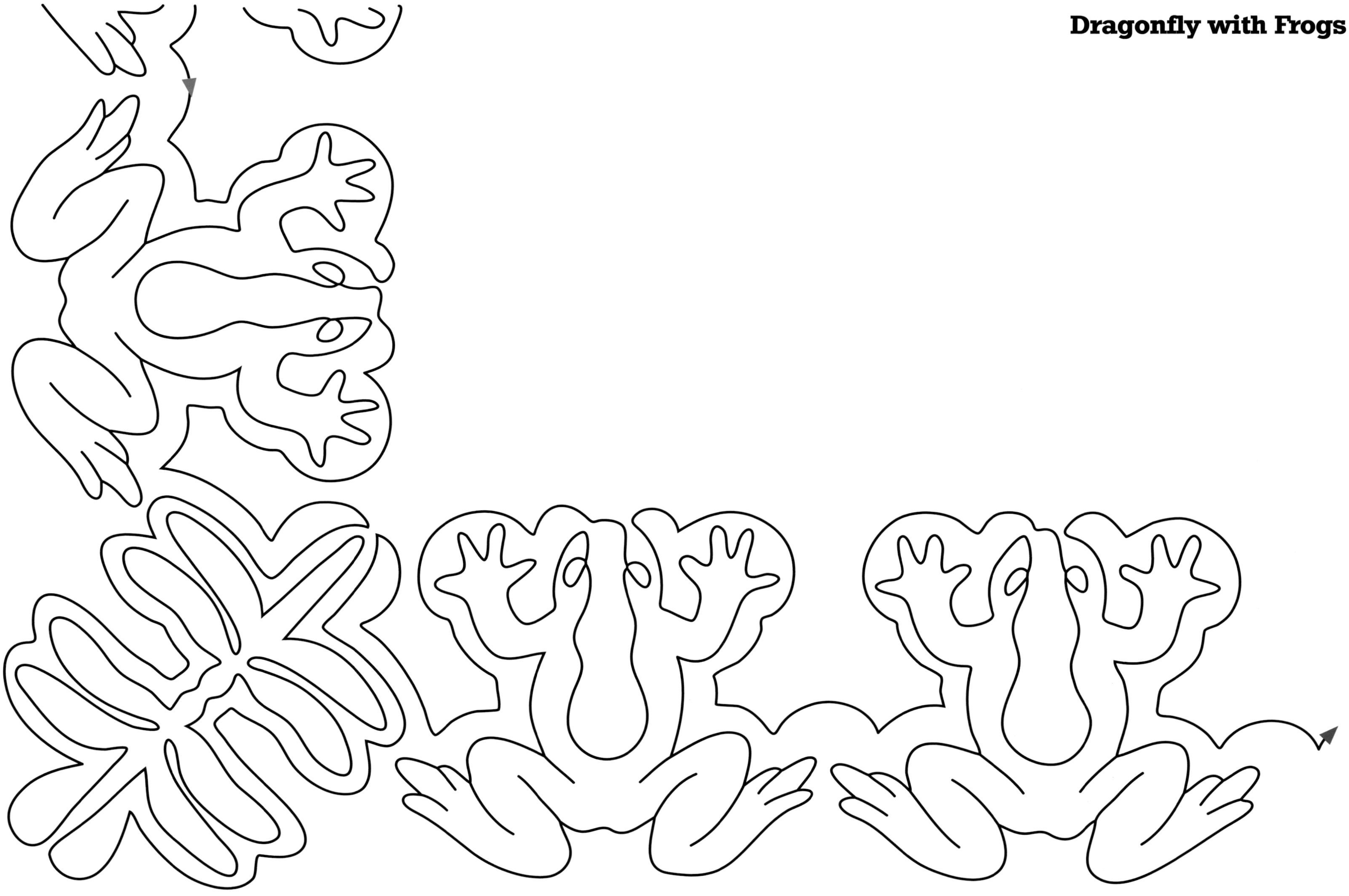

Dragonfly

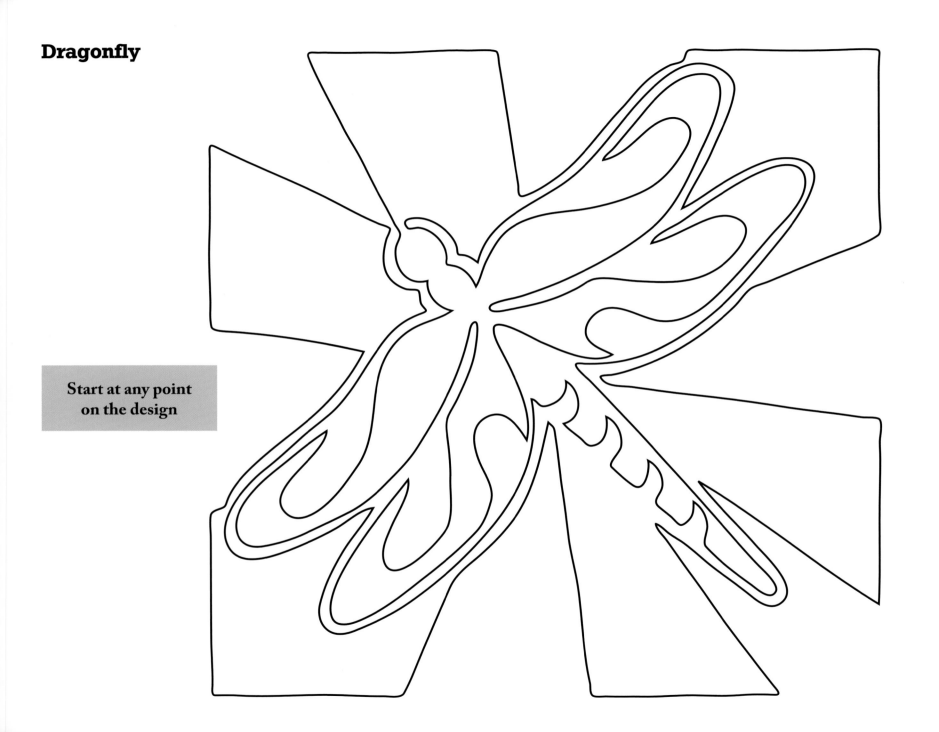

Start at any point
on the design

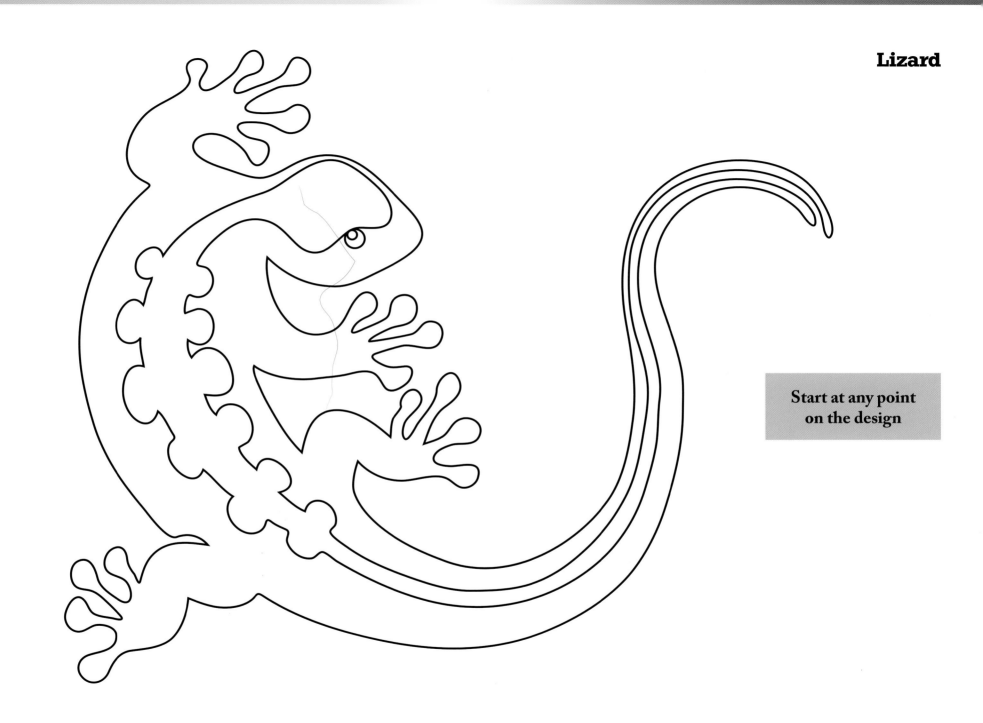

**Start at any point
on the design**

Pond Lily

The Ocean

Create that relaxed feeling in your quilt of a perfect day at the beach—those days with laughter blended with the ripple of the waves.

Seahorse · Fish

Seahorse with Shells

Start at any point on the design

Seahorses with Twirls Block

Start at any point on the design

Seahorses with Twirls Border

Mussel · Seashell

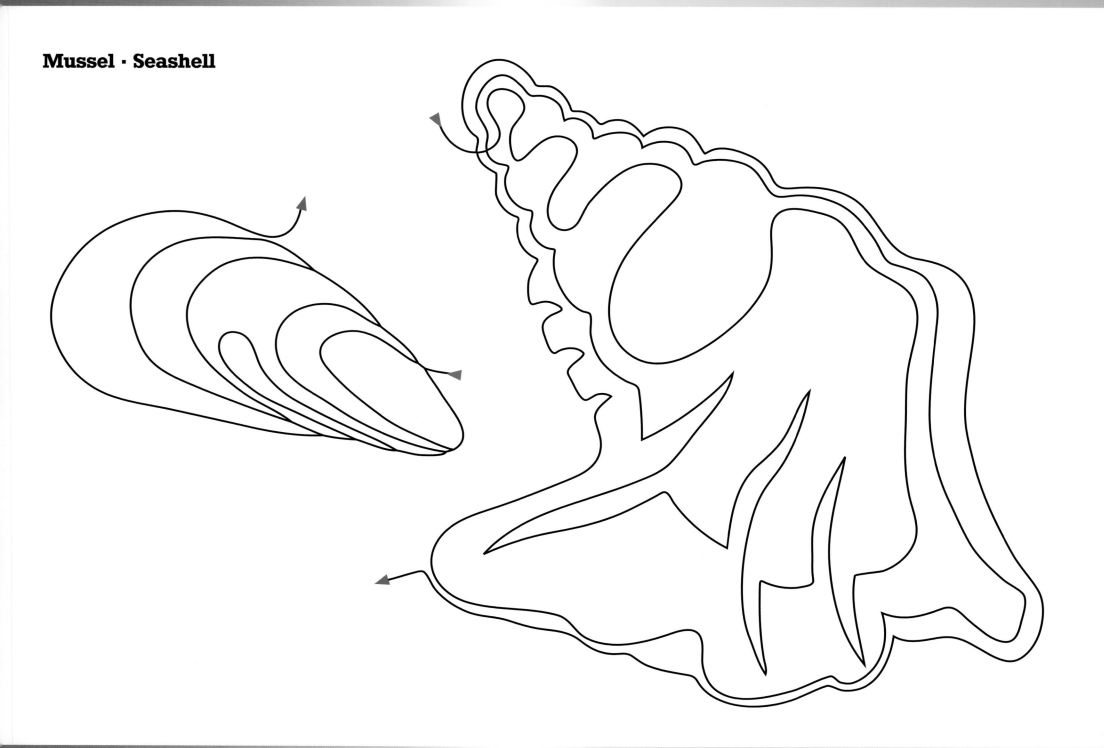

Dolphin

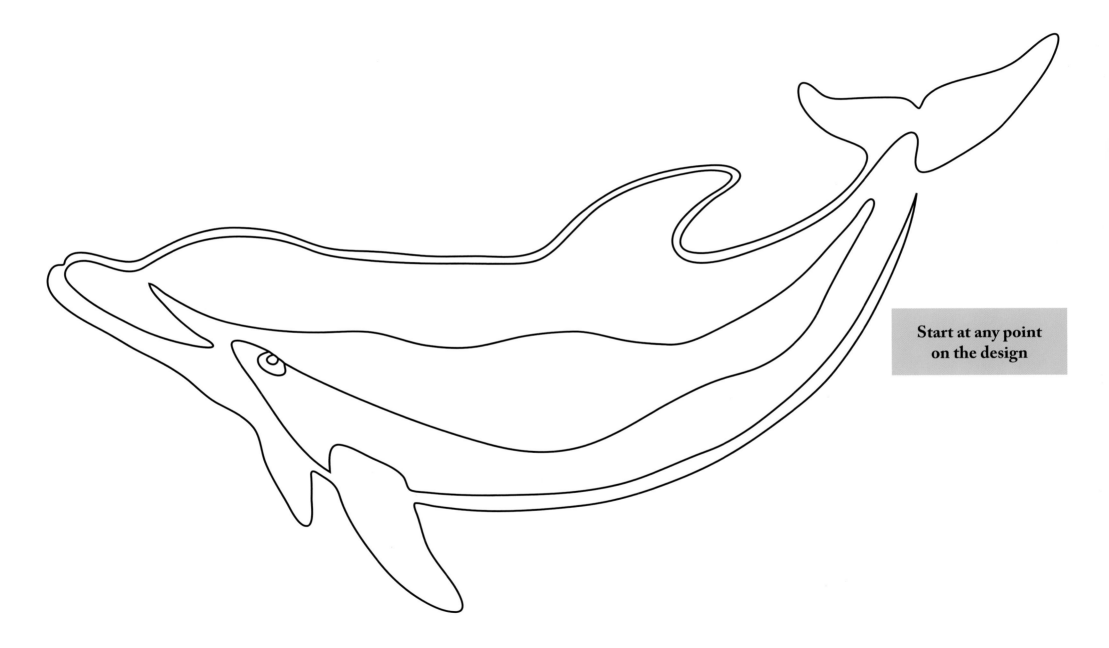

Start at any point
on the design

The Forest

Whether a pair of startled deer or leaves from the majestic oak, the magic of the woods will thrive when stitched onto needlework.

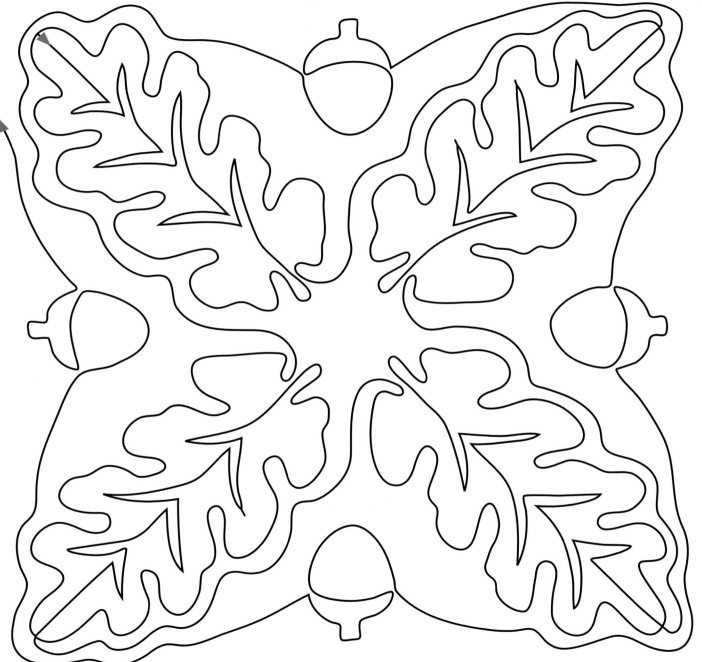

Oak Leaves & Acorn

Beetle · Moth

Oak Leaves & Acorn

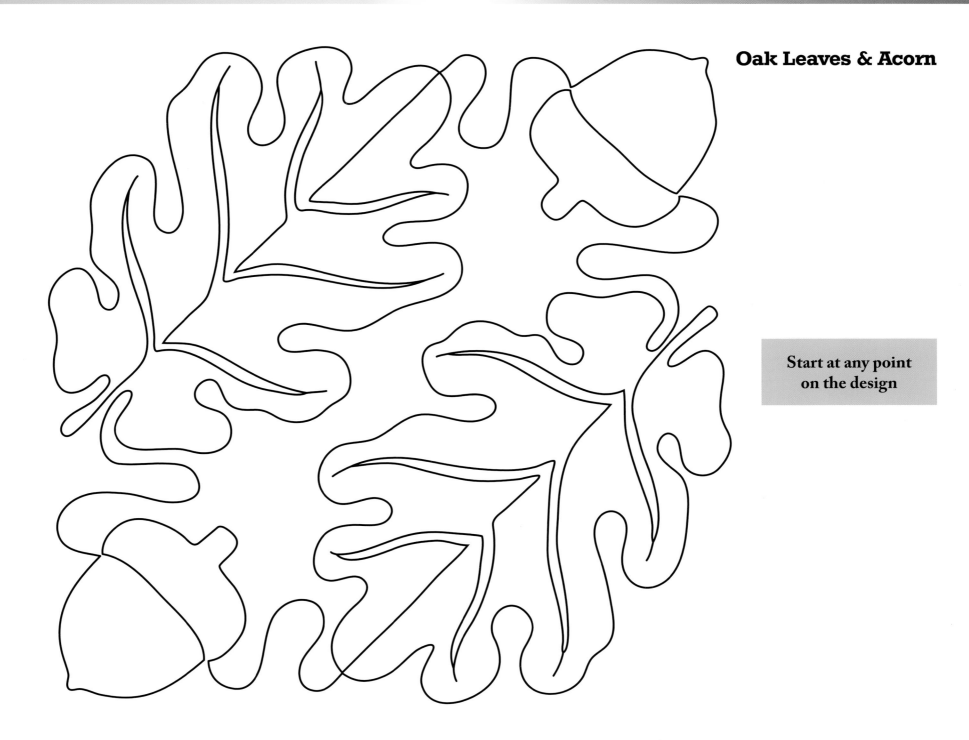

Start at any point
on the design

Mushrooms

Boxing Hares

Deer

The Dogs

These canines will neither scratch your quilt nor leave pesky fur, so go ahead and welcome these mutts all over your patchwork.

Labrador · Dachshund

Chihuahua · Basset Hound

Great Dane

The Birds

Whether as singing silhouettes on blue sky or diving in arctic waters, birds suit quilts like coffee goes with chocolate.

Soaring Eagle

The Flowers

The language of flowers, universal and loving, is sure to enhance your quilt top. Petals and leaves are always a pleasure to find among the geometric shapes of your blocks.

Equestrian

High speed athletes and gentle nickers, the softness of cotton will be a perfect pasture.

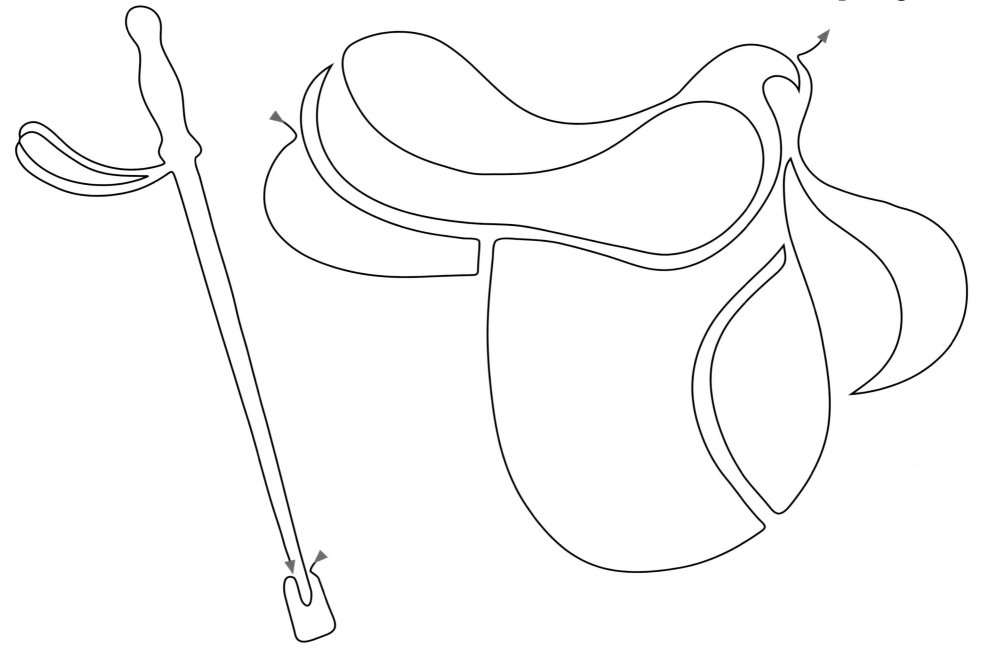

Bridle · English Top Hat

Start at any point
on the design

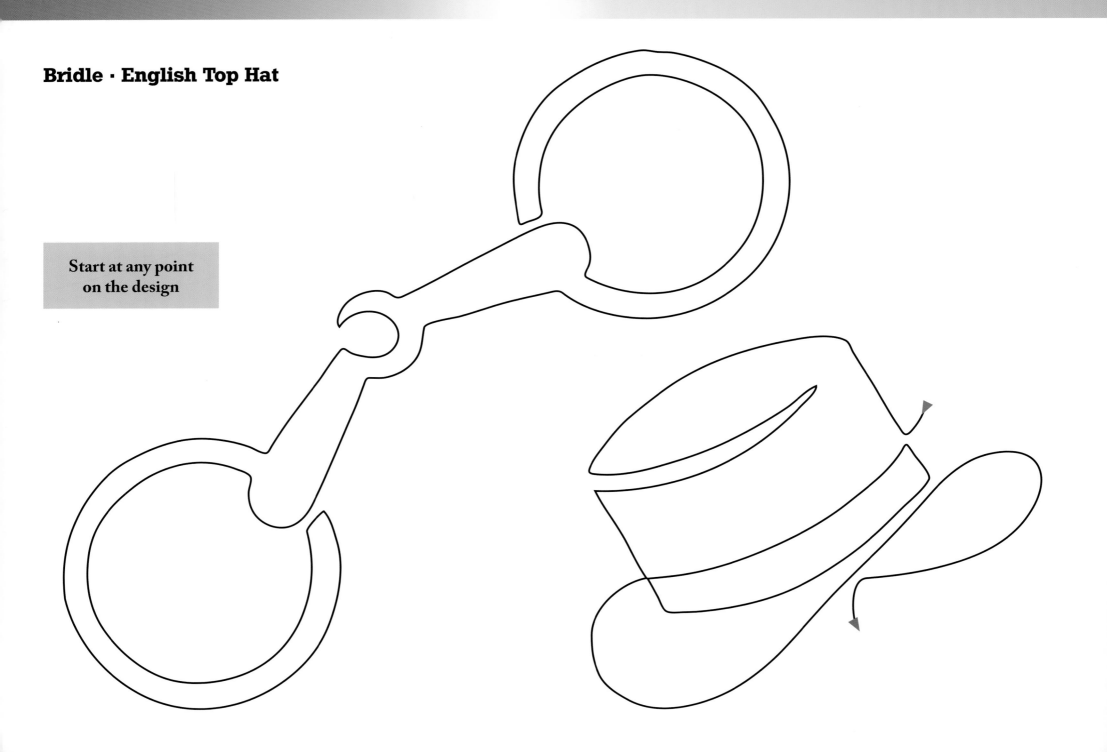

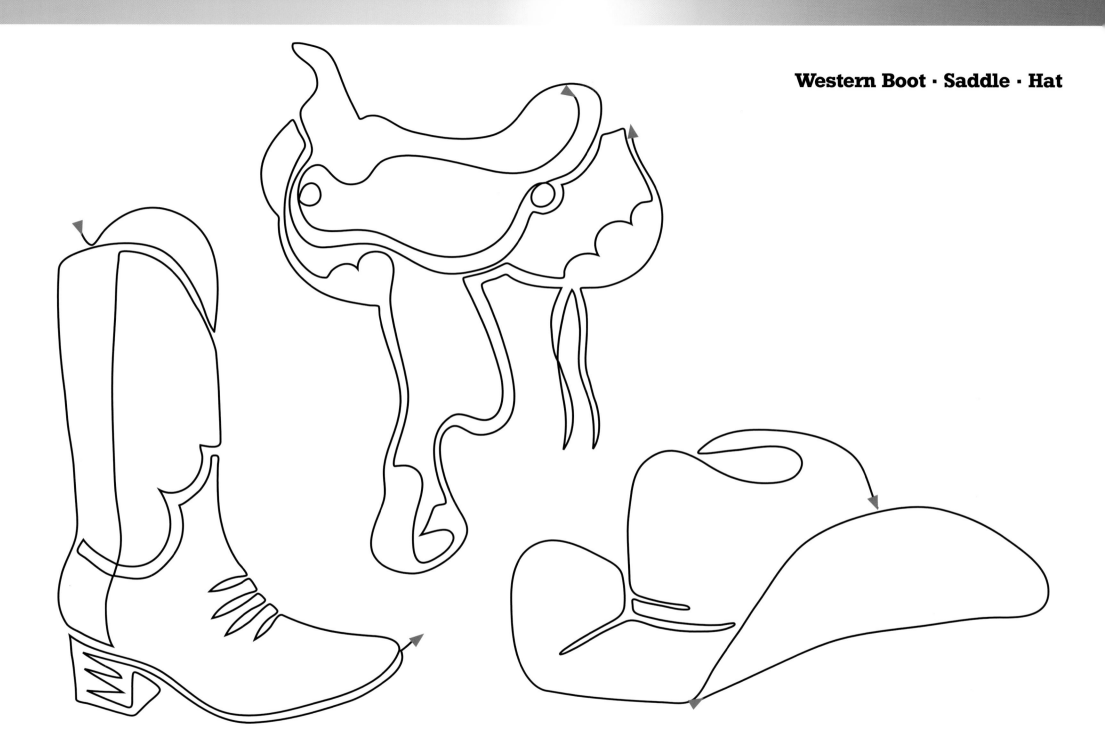

Rearing Horse

Horse Face

Start at any point
on the design

Horse Face/Shoe Border

Dinosaurs, Dragons & More

An eclectic selection of various candies for quilters

Dragon

Use drawings on pages 87–90 for precision when assembling the dragon. This is an illustration to show the finished design.

Dragon Middle

Dragon Tail

Pegasus

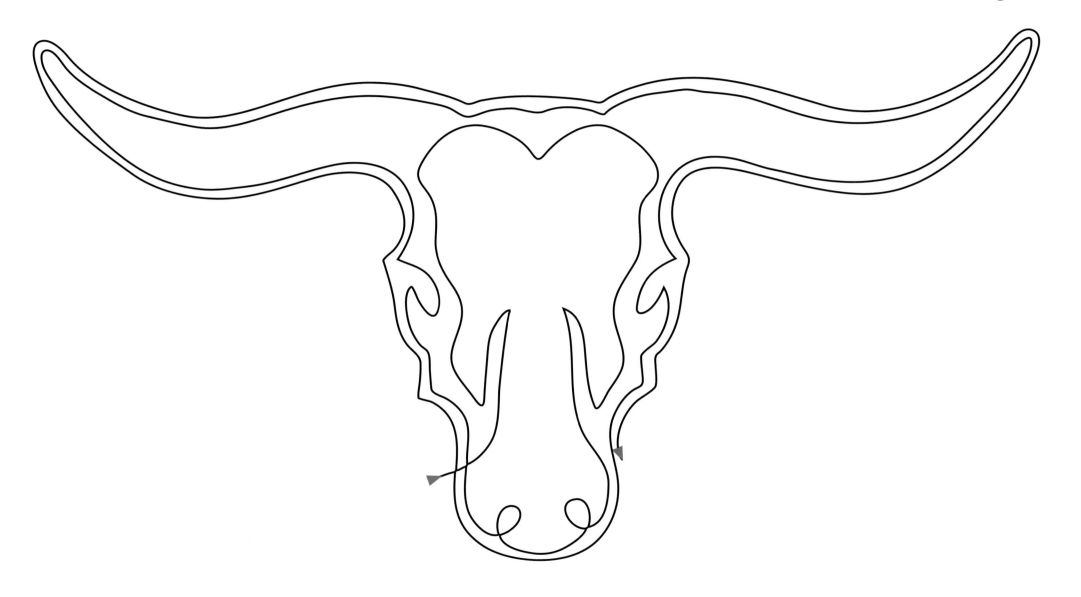

Teapot · Cupcake · Teacup

About the Author

Lone Minkkinen was born and raised in Denmark. As a little girl, she remembers that her mother would sew smartly tailored clothes with attention to every detail. Lone wanted to sew too, but making clothes was not her main interest. She wanted to use the sewing machine for drawing, as the fabrics were so tempting to use as canvasses for high stepping horses and princesses with long black hair.

Her mother told her fabrics were much too expensive to use in that way and if Lone wanted to draw, she could use pencils and paper. And Lone did just that. She drew and drew, and if she ran out of paper, she drew on whatever was available. It didn't take her long to fill up the freshly painted walls of the staircase with dinosaurs as high as a seven-year-old girl could reach with a black permanent marker.

As an adult, her love of drawing and painting led her to become a graphic designer. Later she met her American husband, Jim, with whom she now has two children. When they moved to the United States, Lone became a stay-at-home mom. The following years she would often be seen with a spoon in one hand and a paintbrush in the other.

After purchasing a painting from Lone, a client told her about how she liked to quilt. Not knowing about quilting, but very curious, this led to a delightful introduction of the craft, a new friendship, and Lone's first brand new sewing machine!

Many of the sketches in this book were drawn in her Danish homeland, where she returns each summer. Her cottage there sits on the edge of a forest near the ocean. At night, frogs can be heard from the nearby pond and until mid-July, nightingales sing. Every day Lone and her kids go to the beach, where the children play like otters in the water.

In the light Scandinavian evenings, she and her mom frequently walk the forest trails. The setting sun throws gold and copper on the straight beech tree trunks, making the moss and the gnarly beech tree roots looks like dinosaur toes.

Lone lives in Michigan with her husband and their two children, two dogs, and a cat. This is Lone's first published book.

To contact Lone or to see more of her works, go to her website www.seabrightart.com.

Photo by Linda Michele-Dobel Photography, Brighton, Michigan

More Quilting Design Books from AQS Publishing

This is only a small selection of the books available from the American Quilter's Society. AQS books are available from your local bookseller, quilt shop, or public library.

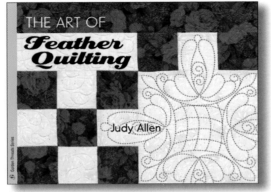

#6678

#6900

#7015

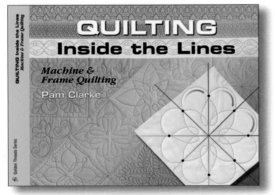

#7072

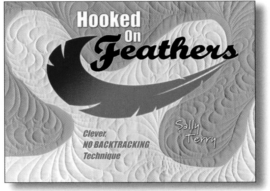

#7732

#8234

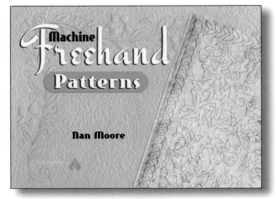

#8022

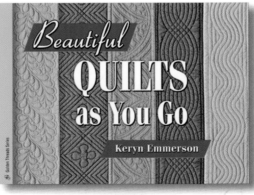

#6803

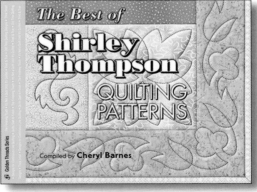

#6571

CALL or **VISIT** our website at **1-800-626-5420** ▪ **www.AmericanQuilter.com**